Congratulations Parents!

Welcome to the *Think You're Smarter Than The Dowe Twins, Learning Through Trivia Activity Workbooks and Flashcards Game Series*! We are excited that you have chosen us as a resource for your child/children's additional educational support. With your purchase, your child/children are now automatically entitled to enroll for FREE into the Dowe Twins Kids Club. To register go to www.DTKC.DoweTwins.com!

Knowing that all children learn differently, and in many cases supplemental materials are needed to help support their academic achievement, *Think You're Smarter Than The Dowe Twins* series is the perfect choice. By using a competition-style component, children at multiple grade levels will be learning some of the fundamental educational subjects in the most fun way possible.

Our workbooks and flashcards series have been carefully created by our team of professionals, who have combined educational facts with custom-designed activities, all intended to help children build their analytical and critical thinking skills.

You are never too young or old to find the excitement in learning, and we are sure there will never be a dull moment. With laughter and shocking finds, the *Think You're Smarter Than The Dowe Twins* workbooks and flashcards game will have children excited about learning through trivia and wanting to learn more!

Let the learning fun begin!


Sincerely,
*The Dowe Family*

Copyright © 2020 by Dowe Twins Company

All rights reserved. In accordance with the U.S. Copyright Act of 1976, the scanning, uploading, and electronic sharing of any part of this book without the permission of the publisher constitutes unlawful piracy and theft of the author's intellectual property. If you would like to use material from the book (other than for review purposes), prior written permission must be obtained by contacting the publisher at info@dowetwins.com

Library of Congress Publication Data Alina K. Dowe, Princeton Dowe and Brazil Dowe Think You're Smarter than the Dowe Twins, Learning Through Trivia Activity Workbook
p.cm- (Learning Through Trivia Activity Workbook)
ISBN-13: 978-1-64483-006-2

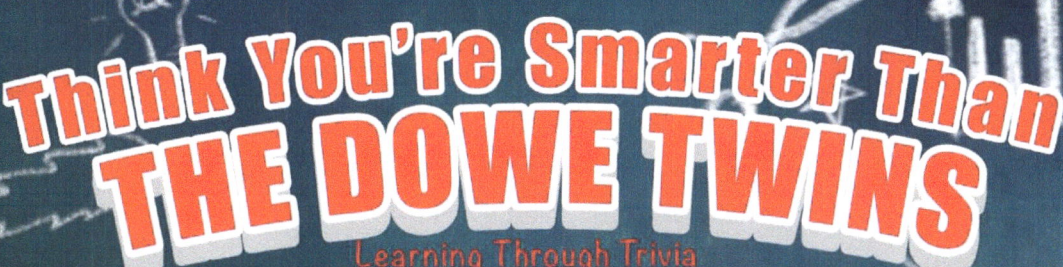

# Think You're Smarter Than THE DOWE TWINS
*Learning Through Trivia Activity Workbook Series*

## Table of Content

Science .................................................................... 4-7

Social Studies ........................................................ 8-11

Language Arts ....................................................... 12-15

Break with Tic Tac Toe ........................................ 16-17

Technology ............................................................ 18-21

Music ...................................................................... 22-25

Art ........................................................................... 26-29

Answer Key ........................................................... 32

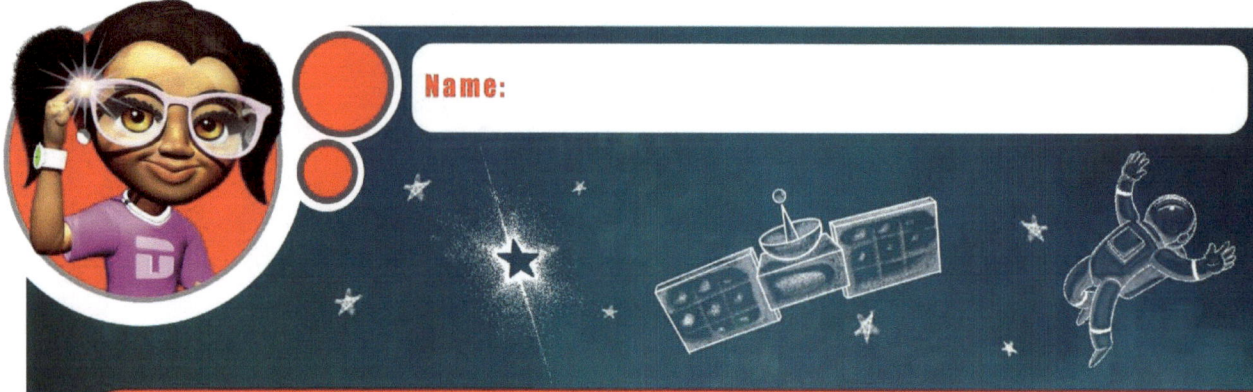

Name:

1. How far is Neptune from the sun?
   A. about 3.7 billion miles
   B. about 4.7 billion miles
   C. about 1.5 billion miles
   D. about 2.8 billion miles

2. A _____ is a huge sphere of very hot, glowing gas.
   A. Moon
   B. Star
   C. Planet
   D. Sun

3. Our solar system is located in the _____.
   A. Black Eye Galaxy
   B. Milky Way Galaxy
   C. Cartwheel Galaxy
   D. Andromeda Galaxy

4. What planet has a great red spot on it?
   A. Jupiter
   B. Saturn
   C. Venus
   D. Pluto

5. What is the blanket of gases surrounding the earth?
   A. Atmosphere
   B. Galaxy
   C. Heaven
   D. Sphere

6. This is a large spacecraft that orbits the earth.
   A. Airplanes
   B. International Space Station
   C. Rockets
   D. Space Exploration

7. A _____ is a place in space where gravity pulls so much that even light can not get out.
   A. White Hole
   B. Black Hole
   C. Universe
   D. Supernova

**Think You're Smarter Than The Dowe Twins**

Name:

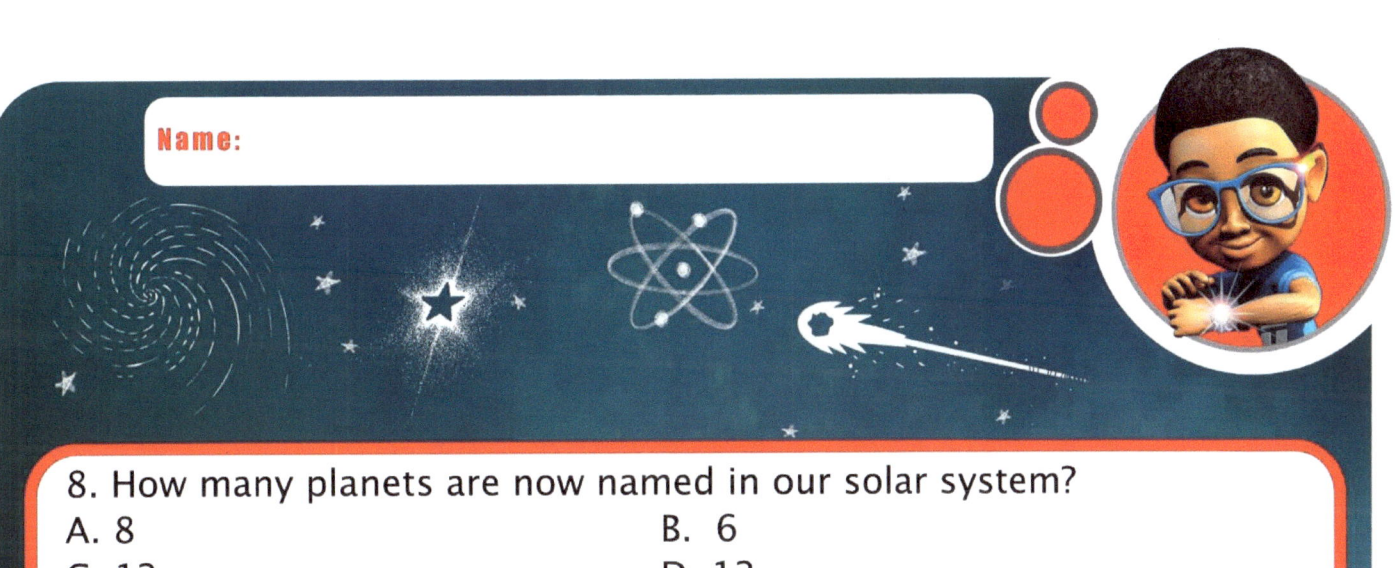

8. How many planets are now named in our solar system?
A. 8
B. 6
C. 12
D. 12

9. What is the third planet from the sun?
A. Mars
B. Earth
C. Venus
D. Saturn

10. What is the hottest planet in the solar system?
A. Mercury
B. Venus
C. Pluto
D. Mars

11. What are the two planets in the solar system that don't have a moon?
A. Mercury and Venus
B. Saturn and Earth
C. Jupiter and Venus
D. Venus and Mars

12. How many Earths can fit in the sun?
A. about 1000 Earths
B. about 500 Earths
C. about 100,000 Earths
D. about 1.3 million Earths

**Learning Through Trivia Activity Workbook**

Name:

# Word Search

Can you find the words in the grid below?

```
D G W T A G I S H U Q L H K R X Z Q
I R V E M S A G I O B S Q O N F M Q
M A Y N A W Z N Q T W K Y E M U S M
S V V F N C V S Y H E L I U M V C N
W I P V A E A T M O S P H E R E N K
I T L I R C P L M E R C U R Y M U E
I Y Y X V S N T H A A T T U Y Z M Y
Y B N X F P W K U P E Z X G C K M H
H Q G X Q M H Y H N G E A R T H B D
D H Y D R O G E N B E R Y I J I N O
A O Z T E L E S C O P E S F X R E Z
C E R B K G Y U E W E X U I C S F E
```

Neptune
Gravity
Atmosphere
Mercury
Telescopes
Hydrogen
Helium
Earth

**Think You're Smarter Than The Dowe Twins**

**Name:**

# Maze

Help the astronaut find the way to the spaceship!

Start

Finish

**Learning Through Trivia Activity Workbook**

Name:

1. Who's the forty-fifth President of the United States?
A. George Washington   B. Donald Trump
C. Barack Obama   D. James Madison

2. What is the name of the first ten amendments of the US Constitution?
A. Legislatures   B. Legal Rights
C. Bill of Rights   D. Rule of Law

3. Who was the first US President?
A. George Washington   B. James Madison
C. Thomas Jefferson   D. Benjamin Franklin

4. What continent is reported to be the largest of the seven?
A. Asia   B. Africa
C. Europe   D. North America

5. Which two countries share the border of the United States of America?
A. Canada and Mexico   B. Mexico and Brazil
C. Canada and South America   D. Cuba and Alaska

6. What is the longest continental mountain range in the world?
A. Himalayan Mountains   B. Andes Mountains
C. The Alps   D. Rocky Mountains

7. What are the three branches of US Government?
  A. Legislative, Congress, Judicial
  B. President, Executive, The Cabinet
  C. Legislative, Executive, Judicial
  D. Supreme Court, Executive, Defense

Think You're Smarter Than The Dowe Twins

Name:

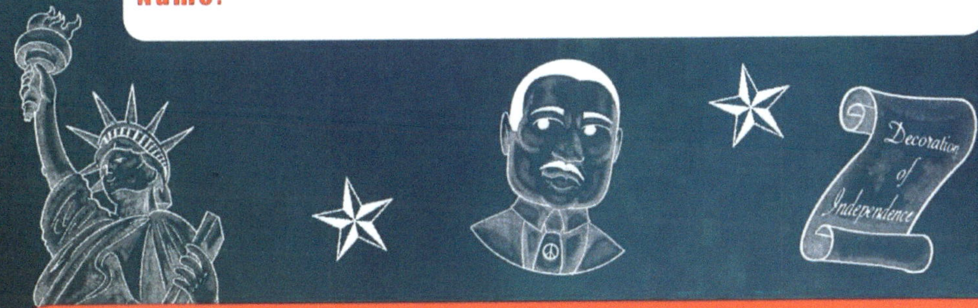

8. How many countries are in North America?
A. 3
B. 23
C. 50
D. 14

9. What is the longest river in the world?
A. Amazon River
B. Nile River
C. Congo River
D. Mississippi River

10. The National Monument where four presidents' faces are carved is called:
A. Mount Rushmore
B. Devils Tower National Monument
C. National Mall
D. Statue of Liberty National Monument

11. Whose face is on the US$20 bill?
A. Abraham Lincoln
B. George Washington
C. Andrew Jackson
D. Bill Clinton

12. How many states are in the United States?
A. 50
B. 49
C. 52
D. 51

Learning Through Trivia Activity Workbook

Name:

# Crack the Code

Using the number codes below, fill in the blanks to reveal the secret message!

| | | |
|---|---|---|
| | | |
| 20 | 8 | 5 |

| | | | | | | | | | | |
|---|---|---|---|---|---|---|---|---|---|---|
| | | | | | | | | | | |
| 4 | 5 | 3 | 12 | 1 | 18 | 1 | 20 | 9 | 15 | 14 |

| | |
|---|---|
| | |
| 15 | 6 |

| | | | | | | | | | | | |
|---|---|---|---|---|---|---|---|---|---|---|---|
| | | | | | | | | | | | |
| 9 | 14 | 4 | 5 | 16 | 5 | 14 | 4 | 5 | 14 | 3 | 5 |

| | | | | | | | | |
|---|---|---|---|---|---|---|---|---|
| A | B | C | D | E | F | G | H | I |
| 1 | 2 | 3 | 4 | 5 | 6 | 7 | 8 | 9 |
| J | K | L | M | N | O | P | Q | R |
| 10 | 11 | 12 | 13 | 14 | 15 | 16 | 17 | 18 |
| S | T | U | V | W | X | Y | Z | |
| 19 | 20 | 21 | 22 | 23 | 24 | 25 | 26 | |

# Do you know who is on the US Bills?

Use the lines under the bills to write the name of the person who's face is on that bill.

_____

_____     _____

_____     _____

**Learning Through Trivia Activity Workbook**

Name:

1. _____ is the action or capability of understanding something.
   A. Knowledge
   B. Apprehension
   C. Perception
   D. Comprehension

2. Coordinating, subordinating and correlative are the three types of _____?
   A. Conjunctions
   B. Affiliations
   C. Agreements
   D. Collaborations

3. What are the two main parts of a sentence?
   A. Structure & Grammar
   B. Subject & Predicate
   C. Statement & Question
   D. Noun & Objective

4. _____ are words that modify (describe) nouns.
   A. Adjectives
   B. Adverbs
   C. Pronouns
   D. Verbs

5. The body of words used in a particular language is called:
   A. Vocabulary
   B. Interjections
   C. Vowel
   D. Novel

6. One or two or more words or expressions of the same language that have the same or nearly the same meaning in some or all senses?
   A. Antonyms
   B. Opposites
   C. Adjective
   D. Synonyms

7. Books and writings published on a particular subject are called:
   A. Literature
   B. Compositions
   C. Preposition
   D. Publication

**Think You're Smarter Than The Dowe Twins**

Name:

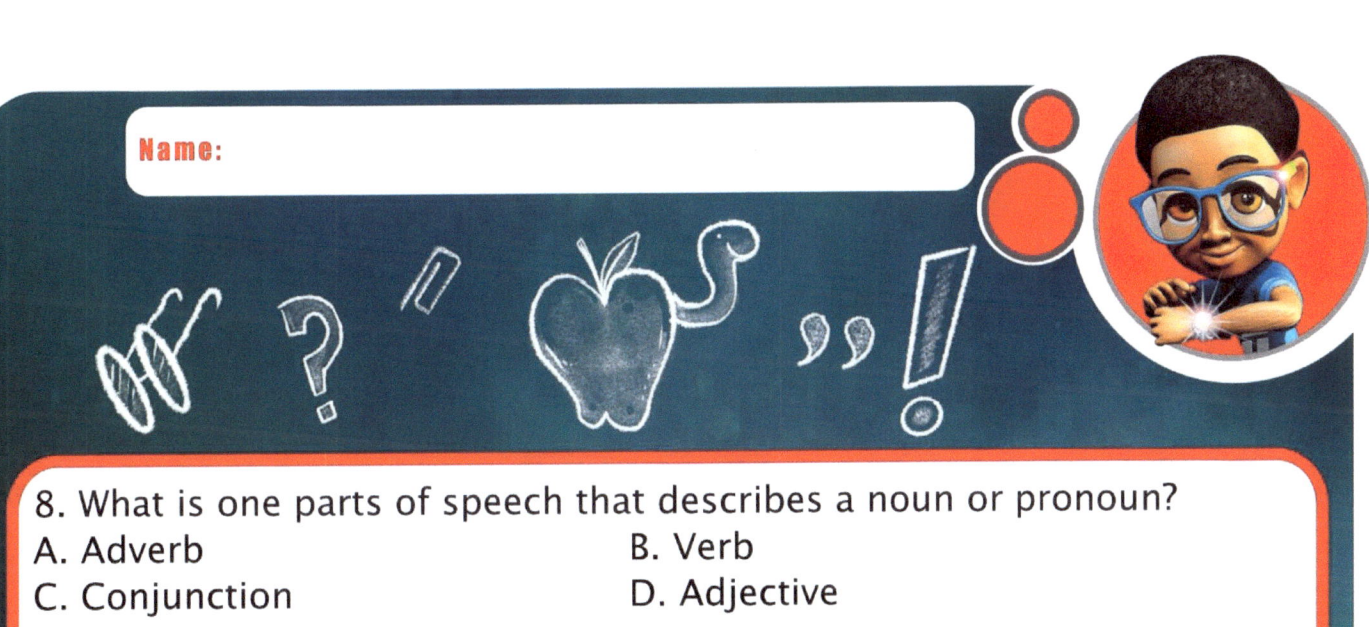

8. What is one parts of speech that describes a noun or pronoun?
A. Adverb
B. Verb
C. Conjunction
D. Adjective

9. A shortened form of words or phrases that can be read as a word is called:
A. Suffix
B. Acronym
C. Prefix
D. Sounds

10. A distinct section of writing covering one topic is called:
A. Sentence
B. Paper
C. Story
D. Paragraph

11. This is a word that is pronounced the same as another word but has a different meaning and/or spelling.
A. Homophone
B. Homographs
C. Conjunction
D. Consonant

12. What is literature that is based on facts and real events?
A. Nonfactual
B. Nonfiction
C. Fiction
D. Factual

Name:

# Word Search

Can you find the words in the grid below?

```
H I U J S X M O S I U P P D H V B I
P O Y H B E F A E P Y U R H N O B F
F A R M M E Y K V N T U B O Z O W P V
E C M O V N U C T I F L N M N E U W
H F R T P F N S E W W I O I F L I F
A V O O Z H A D N B X C U J I I F Z
U K T Y N Q O U C H U A N I C Y U D
L S A U R Y M N E H E T I G T G J A
I L E G S X M N E L M I F X I S B E
C O M P R E H E N S I O N E O K G R
G A X J S L C L F D W N V J N Q V D
O U L O O S I F P R E E Q Z N M R G
```

ACRONYM
COMPREHENSION
HOMOPHONE
NONFICTION
PRONOUN
PUBLICATION
SENTENCE
VOWEL

**Think You're Smarter Than The Dowe Twins**

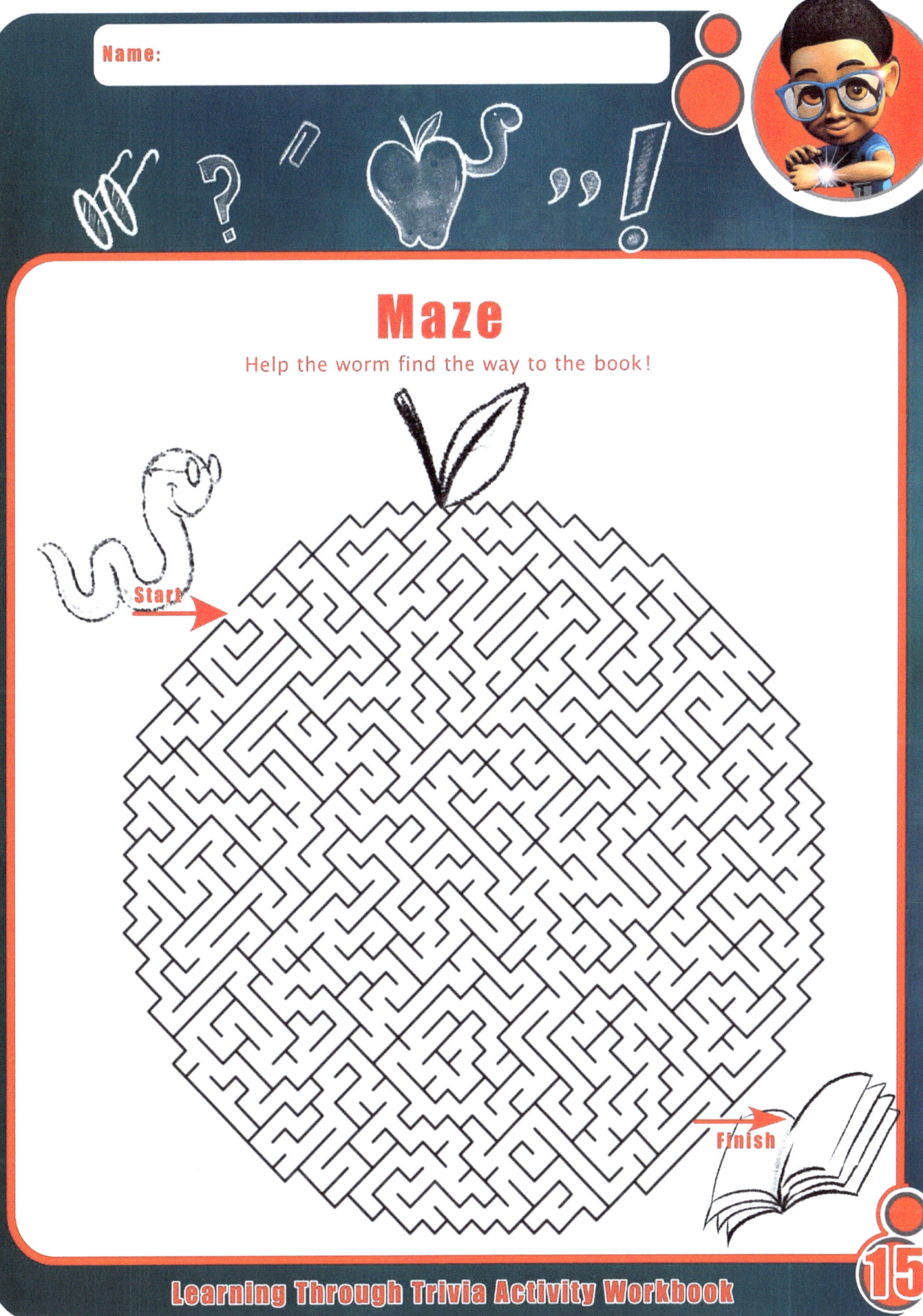

Name:

1. A type of software that allows you to perform specific tasks is called:
A. System
B. App
C. Machine
D. Data

2. This refers to the physical parts of a computer.
A. Software
B. Application
C. Hardware
D. Motherboard

3. What is a location or address identifying where documents can be found on the Internet?
A. DNS
B. API
C. BSS
D. URL

4. The study of computers and computational systems is called:
A. Processor
B. Computer Science
C. Data Analysis
D. Programming

5. This is an application used to access and view websites.
A. Router
B. Network
C. Modem
D. Web Browser

6. A global network of billions of computers and other electronic devices.
A. Mainframe
B. Database
C. Internet
D. Google

7. A person who writes computer programs is a:
A. Computer Coder
B. Computer Programmer
C. Computer Engineer
D. Computer Creator

**Think You're Smarter Than The Dowe Twins**

Name:

8. Paul Allen and Bill Gates were the founders of _____.
A. Apple	B. Cisco
C. Microsoft	D. Facebook

9. What does CPU stand for in computers?
A. Computer Power User	B. Cost Per Unit
C. Corel Power User	D. Central Processing Unit

10. The first workable prototype of the internet came in what year?
A. 1980	B. 2000
C. 1990	D. 1960

11. The system of sending written messages electronically from one computer to another is:
A. Texting	B. Emailing
C. Coding	D. Twitting

12. What is it called when using electronic communication to bully a person?
A. Cyberbullying	B. Cyber Warfare
C. Cyber Terrorism	D. Cyberpunk

Learning Through Trivia Activity Workbook

# Crack the Code

Using the symbol codes below, fill in the blanks to reveal the secret message!

▷◻◻◻◁▱◥   ◥◯△◯▷◻▷◥

▱◻   ◥▽◯   ▱◯◻

### Code Key:

| a | b | c | d | e | f | g | h | i | j | k | l | m | n | o | p |
|---|---|---|---|---|---|---|---|---|---|---|---|---|---|---|---|
| ◻ | ◇ | △ | ▱ | ◯ | ▱ | ◥ | ⋈ | ▷ | ◁ | ▽ | ▷ | △ | ◁ | ◯ | ▽ |

| q | r | s | t | u | v | w | x | y | z |
|---|---|---|---|---|---|---|---|---|---|
| ▽ | ◻ | ◯ | ▱ | ⩍ | ⋈ | ⋈ | ◁ | △ | ◯ |

Name:

# Name the hardware
Use the lines to write the name of the computer hardware.

1. _____

2. _____

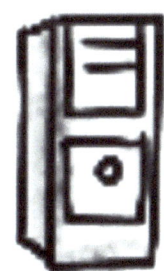

3. _____

4. _____

5. _____

6. _____

Name:

1. The highest of the four standard singing voices is:
A. Mezzo-Soprano
B. Soprano
C. Bass
D. Baritone

2. A _____ is a group of musicians that works together to perform music.
A. Mob
B. Gang
C. Band
D. Troupe

3. How many different genres and sub-genres of music are there?
A. About 1200
B. About 10
C. About 500
D. About 50

4. The trumpet belongs to what musical family?
A. Brass
B. Percussion
C. Woodwind
D. Strings

5. How many people are in a duet?
A. 3
B. 2
C. 5
D. 10

6. A group of musicians, dancers, or actors who perform together is called a:
A. Performance
B. Symphony
C. Instruments
D. Ensemble

7. Nashville, Tennessee is best known as the home of _____ music.
A. Heavy Metal
B. Country
C. Jazz
D. Folk

**Think You're Smarter Than The Dowe Twins**

8. This place is said to be the birth place of hip hop.
A. Atlanta
B. Brooklyn
C. The Bronx
D. Los Angeles

9. Tempo is the _____ of music.
A. Beats
B. Speed
C. Counts
D. Time

10. What instruments are most associated with rock and roll music?
A. Electric Guitar
B. Drums
C. Bass
D. All of the above

11. This genre of music is named after a color.
A. Reds Music
B. Pinks Music
C. Blues Music
D. Purples Music

12. In music, the acronym for " DJ" means:
A. Dinner Jockey
B. Desk Jockey
C. Disc Jockey
D. Digital Jockey

Learning Through Trivia Activity Workbook

Name:

# Word Search

Can you find the words in the grid below?

```
H B I E N S E M B L E L S M E Z K R
R G I N S T R U M E N T S A D X J J
Z D R M N O M L H W O O D W I N D E
N L D G X M M R S P N N B T M R U S
R D C A L O P R S W M O T L K O M O
V Q Y O T K E B G Y A N B L U J M P
X F M U R J P B V G I X L P S E S R
G S B T L V K E X E M Z J V M A S A
S V A Y S U J P A M U K C F P L M N
S Y S B P E R F O R M A N C E L G O
C R S S P E R C U S S I O N F V S K
R H I X G L N V F P H U L D C A E S
```

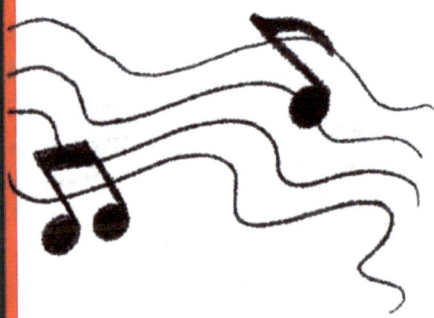

Soprano
Bass
Percussion
Woodwind
Performance
Instruments
Ensemble
Blues

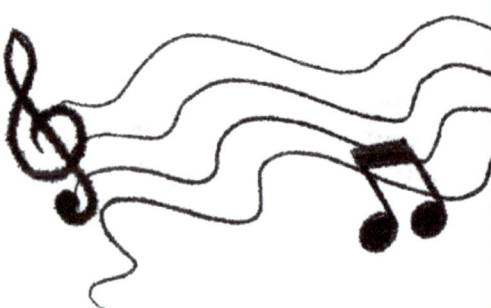

Think You're Smarter Than The Dowe Twins

# Maze

Help Beethoven find his way to the piano!

Name:

1. This is art created with pieces of paper, photographs, fabric and other objects that are arranged and stuck down onto a supporting surface.
A. Collection					B. Composition
C. Collage					D. Collective

2. _____ colors cannot be mixed from other colors.
A. Pastel					B. Primary
C. Complementary				D. Neutral

3. The Mona Lisa, one of the most famous painting in the world, was painted by:
A. Salvador Dali				B. Leonardo da Vinci
C. James McNeil Whistler			D. Vincent Van Gogh

4. A professional that focuses on the art of capturing images electronically is a:
A. Photographer				B. Videographer
C. Director					D. Producer

5. The art that depends on motion for its effect is called:
A. Kinetic Art					B. Abstract Art
C. Modern Art					D. Realism Art

6. A _____ is responsible for the recording of live events as well as smaller scale editing and video productions.
A. Screenwriter				B. Director
C. Videographer				D. Photographer

7. What two primary colors make a secondary color?
A. Yellow + Blue = Purple			B. Blue + Red = Green
C. Red + Yellow = Orange			D. Black + White = Gray

Think You're Smarter Than The Dowe Twins

Name:

8. _____ tells stories, or reports on people and events, visually through photographs.
   A. Photojournalism
   B. Formalism
   C. Cinematography
   D. Freelancer

9. A photograph taken by oneself on a smartphone or webcam is a:
   A. Snapshot
   B. Elsie
   C. Youie
   D. Selfie

10. A _____ is a painting, drawing, photograph, or engraving of a person.
    A. Artwork
    B. Picture
    C. Portrait
    D. Sculpture

11. Adding black to a color to make it darker creates a _____.
    A. Tint
    B. Shade
    C. Layer
    D. Outline

12. _____ is modern art that does not represent images of our everyday world.
    A. Abstract Art
    B. Expression Art
    C. Realistic Art
    D. Outsider Art

**Learning Through Trivia Activity Workbook**

Name:

**CREATE YOUR OWN ABSTRACT ARTWORK**

# CERTIFICATE OF ACHIEVEMENT

## THIS AWARD IS PRESENTED TO:

FOR COMPLETING THE "THINK YOU'RE SMARTER THAN THE DOWE TWINS" TRIVIA WORKBOOK!

DATE

SIGNED

You are now an official member of The Dowe Twins Kids Club!

**THE DOWE TWINS**
www.DOWETWINS.com

## ABOUT THE AUTHORS

The "*Think You're Smarter Than the Dowe Twins, Learning Through Trivia, Workbooks and Flashcard Games Series,* was created during the 2020 Coronavirus Worldwide Pandemic, by Alina K. Dowe, MBA, Princeton Dowe and Brazil Dowe, a family no strangers to adversity.

After giving birth to extremely preterm babies, Alina and her husband knew their lives would take on a different journey. But it wasn't until the twins started elementary school did it become apparent that learning really doesn't come so easily for all children. The twins would prove to be a great example of how parents need to get creative in order to support in their child's academic achievements.

While Alina would learn that her children were dealing with what she calls "unidentifiable disabilities," she realized that the extra support children need is imperative and widespread. This couldn't be more important during this unforeseen crisis. With great respect for teachers and educators all around the world, it couldn't be more obvious that it takes full collaborative efforts between parents, caregivers and educators to ensure the greatest outcome for academic development.

Becoming authors out of necessity, the Dowe family believes educational support that motivates, encourages, challenges, and brings excitement is a prefect formula for assisting children at all levels in learning.

With input from Princeton and Brazil **Dowe** (aka The Dowe Twins), with guidance from Professor B. Brown, M.S.-Early Childhood Education, college professor, 20 years homeschool educator and mother of five; Ms. R. Newbold, M.A./TSHH; T.K. Butler-Likely, PhD, editor and proofreader; Steve Cas, Marvel, digital illustrator, 3D modeler and Disney licensed artist; and Angelo C. Petullo, BFA, designer and illustrator, *the Think You're Smarter Than The Dowe Twins, Learning Through Trivia series* is now a reality.

**Think You're Smarter Than THE DOWE TWINS**
Learning Through Trivia
Activity Workbook Series

# ANSWER KEY

| Page 4 | Page 5 | Page 8 | Page 9 |
|---|---|---|---|
| 1. D | 8. A | 1. B | 8. B |
| 2. B | 9. B | 2. C | 9. B |
| 3. B | 10. B | 3. A | 10. A |
| 4. A | 11. A | 4. A | 11. C |
| 5. A | 12. D | 5. A | 12. A |
| 6. B | | 6. B | |
| 7. B | | 7. C | |

## Page 10
The Declaration of Independence

## Page 11
$1- Washington, $5- Lincoln, $10- Hamilton, $50- Grant, $100-Franklin

| Page 12 | Page 13 | Page 18 | Page 19 |
|---|---|---|---|
| 1. D | 8. D | 1. B | 8. C |
| 2. A | 9. B | 2. C | 9. D |
| 3. B | 10. D | 3. D | 10. D |
| 4. A | 11. A | 4. B | 11. B |
| 5. A | 12. B | 5. D | 12. A |
| 6. D | | 6. C | |
| 7. A | | 7. B | |

## Page 20
Learning technology is the key

## Page 21
1. Monitor, 2. CPU, 3. Keyboard, 4. Webcam, 5. Mouse, 6. Flash Driver

| Page 22 | Page 23 | Page 26 | Page 27 |
|---|---|---|---|
| 1. B | 8. A | 1. C | 8. A |
| 2. C | 9. B | 2. B | 9. D |
| 3. A | 10. D | 3. B | 10. D |
| 4. A | 11. C | 4. A | 11. B |
| 5. B | 12. C | 5. A | 12. A |
| 6. D | | 6. C | |
| 7. B | | 7. C | |

www.ingramcontent.com/pod-product-compliance
Lightning Source LLC
Chambersburg PA
CBHW061401090426
42743CB00002B/98